Disaster Insurance

Lee Goffin-Bonenfant

BookLeaf Publishing

Presentation by *BookLeaf Publishing*

Web: www.bookleafpub.com

E-mail: info@bookleafpub.com

ISBN: 9789357748094

First edition 2023

For Us.

ACKNOWLEDGEMENT

I want to thank my friends. A life without them would be a life unflavored, and unrecognizable as I'd know what had been lost.

I want to thank a guy, for letting me fall in love with him, and embarrass myself on paper about it.

I want to thank my parents, be they here or annoyingly absent.

I want to thank my cat, because all writers should have a cat as it works with the aesthetic.

I want to thank myself. I tried really hard, so if you don't like my poems, keep it to yourself.
If you must confront me, please lie.

PREFACE

I wrote these poems in late winter, sitting in my car, parked in a beach lot, looking at the waves. I actually hope you don't read this, so it doesn't color your relationship to the work. What I meant to say was that I was nowhere, doing nothing, while having no relationship to chairs or gravity. Try to do the same while reading this.

Disaster Insurance

I know you come from a good place
One with trees, almost fully grown,
That you painstakingly planted
After tilling ash from the ground
Of all the presumptions you watched burn.
But my land is uncultivated
And in a different climate zone.
So while disasters may befall me
They will not be yours
And you cannot prepare me
For the unknown.

Comparative Literature

6 is too many,
      But seven's too few
I'd invite you to stay
      But you're wearing all blue
Which was yesterday's color
      Today's a new hue
Because 6 is too many
      But seven's too few

Eleven is early
      But 3 is too late
You should have arrived
      On an earlier date
With less in your bowl
      And more on your plate
When eleven is early
      But 3 is too late

1 is the truth,
      While two is a lie
If you're skipping stones
      When I'm learning to fly
The body eternal
      Will watch the mind die
For 1 is the truth
      While two is a lie

20/20

I think of vision
And how far we both can see
Forgetting often
That others use glasses like water

One of the frigid times we spent
Looking from different angles
At the same view
You pointed to something in the distance
And asked if it was the town
    Where we wore seasonably inappropriate clothing
    Dressing up as the idealized version of ourselves
I said "Oh that? I don't know."

You held my hand over all the
Things that divide us
    {real; imagined}
    {tangible; poetic}
"I'm just happy you can see it."

The bespectacled balked when I
Told them how soon you said
You were not married to your hometown
But I never wanted to be the other woman

I forget which one is nearsighted,
Because I do not have to know

Trompe-L'œil

5

If I relax my gaze
I would swear there is hope between
The leaves of the sand dusted bushes
Along the path that leads down to the beach
Where you took me the first time
I tucked my head into your chest
And asked you, sheepishly,
To protect the soft skin on my face
From the tempestuous breezes for which I,
In my California hubris,
Was unprepared

Waiting

Living in the moment,
       Like looking at centuries old art
       Hanging on the wall of an esteemed museum
       Depicting iconography of someone else's G-d
       Scrunching my face into inquisitivity
       While a stranger cries as another one
       Passes without looking up
       Wondering how long I should stay in reverence
       And realizing, mid thought,
       That it only matters
To me.

{forgive us}

The poem was already written
        The one I want to write today
Conceived and birthed in my lifetime
        In quicker time than I can learn
Some words of self-admittance
        Some words of dismay
To take the symbol, leave the rhyme
        Feeling paper fingers burn

Sometimes all the words are new
        Sometimes thoughts are all the same
Relaying pattern recognition
        To ask someone new to know
The wrong conclusions that you drew
        Wrong wars waged in wronger name
The dulcet lull of self-attrition
        The sharp frozen glassy glow

This one did the thing I lack
        Spoke words I could not find
Breathed life into the awful death
        And death into facade
Forward, up and down, and back
        Broke what I opined
When I have learned to save my breath
        And let myself be awed

How I Want To Remember It

8

people who knew
Within a week of meeting their
partners
That they would

the dishes in the next room
first meal

And chided myself out loud
Every time I tried to
micromanage

I made brussel sprouts
Because you said you liked them

I said yes, with conviction

The people in the stories I read talked about

Staring at each other across a party

I'm not sure what week it is
                time has   moved
            Erratically when you are around
Technically, we liked each other's faces

I am writing this in case
        One day
                (the same reason   )
I want to be able to remind both of us
        That   I knew

            to kiss you

Spare Me

Did I have to know
      Could I have been lied to forever
It would have been a burden
      But for somebody else
Not me

Every Day

Everyday, which is long
For the rest of my life, which is short

The upkeep is arduous

I am expected to maintain
       While improving
       While practicing
       While never slinking backwards
I am expected to try hard
       For the first time
       For something new
       For the millionth time
I am expected to add
       Something new
       Something old but in a new way
       Something current but with different eyes

The upkeep is arduous

Everyday, which is long
For the rest of my life, which is so very short

Assumptions

For the first time it occurred to me
　　　　That your love is not a given
I had thought it might be true
　　　　But this time my bones
　　　　　　Told my chest
Who whispered to my stomach
　　　　Who blushed
Embarrassed by her own naiveté

For the first time in my many but not too many years
I learned I could be the cause
　　　　Without being the problem
Because I have always been the problem
There are impasses more often that I had assumed
But I had forgotten they don't show up
　　　　Like care instructions

For the first time since I gave up love
　　　　And then, years later, drinking
(I made better choices)
I didn't dive face first into the spiral
Instead I reminded myself
That there will always be reasons
For you not to love me
But the choice to continue

Ah, yes.
There is the love

Spacial Relationships

I am learning to exist
Outside of loneliness
At the point where our
      Lines intersect
I have been round for so long
You are teaching me
      How to be infinite

A Visitor

Time knocked on my door
It had been just over a year since her last visit
There were no pleasantries
        (there never are)
Even though the snow outside
Had recently turned to slush
She did not remove her boots

She lit a cigarette, tossing the match on the hardwood
        Leaving another pock mark
"Tsk tsk tsk"
She said, knocking kitsch, seemingly at random
(precious to some)
        Onto the floor
"So much clutter"
She put her car keys through the glass
        Of a family photo
In which I am the only one (left)
        Still alive

"How do you live like this?"
Tracking sludge and ash throughout the house
I, as always when she comes around,
        Was too stunned to speak
How could she make such a mess so quickly?

She looked around with disappointment
Either in me, or that there wasn't more to break
"I guess I'll see you soon"
       When
"Next time I'm in town"
She left the door ajar
       And I spent the next half hour
Corralling my cat back inside
And the half hour after that
       Sweeping glass and debris
Miserable at the thought of her
Speeding through stop signs

Don't

But what if I do want
To get carried away
By an updraft
Lifting me off the beach
From the bayside
To the sea
Carrying me over
The ripples it makes in the waves?

Wear and Tear

There is loss, of course,
But that assumes I have had anything
Nothing is mine, I am exasperated
Unsure why I want
Like that

To keep it
To trade it in for something else to keep

Floating in and out of other's lives
Floating in and out of mine
I ask them to keep me
      Even though I do not want that
Become irate
      When they will not

I can't be held
While I only exist in time
Which haven't figured out how to walk through
Even though I'm sure it's no more difficult
Than walking through sand
I do not wish to keep the sand

I know that it is a silly thing to want
Clinging to me when it desires

Washing away down the broken
Shells in my driveway when it doesn't

My house, my driveway, isn't even mine
            (my mother's; the markets')
And the parts inside are temporary, still
            The sheets wear
            The door needs new paint
            The 2nd cat scratches the furniture raw
            The milk leaves rotten either way

Permanence is so limited by witness
I invent those witnesses
For what I don't expect to see

I need not be seen
In order to have existed
There is loss, of course
But nothing was ever mine

3 Hours

I try to explain to you that time
Is not fixed
Not in that way, at least.
Without look up form the cloth
Of wood stain you are running over
The hilt of the ax
Head you spent (what seemed like)
Hours sharpening against a wet stone
In the peekaboo daylight.
You say "Yes, my love
Like everything else, it is relative."

I take this as the camaraderie you offer;
As an open side flap of your jacket
In disappearing winter.
That is why I don't feel new,
All shaky newborn deer legs
And sensory overload.
I am a long trip home
And you are shoes kicked off in the doorway.

Steerage

It is an unnatural thing
In the way we define things as unnatural
To,
      From this angle
      At this height
Spend this long watching the light fade
Letting two such miracles
Become ordinary

Of course it's terrifying
      It should be
We were not equipped to look down
Even synthetically
Strapped like cargo
      To the (fever dream) (bright idea)
Of three raccoons in a trenchcoat

Existing on the constant precipice of newness
Allowing for today's dismissal and shun
Of yesterday's impossible victory

For which we should be grateful
For which we should mourn
All (well, some of) the ancestors who did not live to see
      This

But that Kaddish is airborne
And comes for us all
For we too will miss
        Miracles turned mundane
In what was never meant to be
Our lifetimes

And the dwelling of,
        Like Little Prince sunsets
        Seen from space
Turns from dismissal to dismissal
What should awestrike
What should leave breathless
Before it, too, devolves into natural

Walls

You remark how tall
The shadow I cast seems to you but
    I see the oblong
    I see the distortion
    I see how the sausage is made
Staring at my three dee sneakers
Against my greyscale platonic facsimile
I know I am a lie
But it seems lost on you that your shadow
Strange and malformed as it may be
Is holding assumed silhouetted hands
With mine

Habits

We are a snowball three quarters of the way
down the mountain
Gaining speed and traction
Only now asking
Who might be at the bottom
Too late, my friend
We have been let loose
We have let ourselves loose
We have let ourselves go
All dumpy between the ears, fatty and delicious
Not round, swelling with love
Rosy cheeked in the crisp air
We have spun into ourselves
Black holes for our own assurity

It must be true, if it already is.
It must have already been done.

Mortification

Try to remember
No one is thinking about you
Mostly
        Except that one time you fell
        In college
        In front of everyone staring out
        From the cafeteria fishbowl
        Watching you lay in resignation
        Just a beat too long
        On the melting slush
        Because you wore the wrong shoes
                Erica reminds you often
                That even if she didn't know you
                Even if she hadn't promised
                To let you give her children
                A Jewish Education
                She would have remembered
                Letting out a laugh
                When you finally
                After internal eons
                Stood up.

Fin

Seven women kick their heads back in laughter,
Breathless.
"I remember being born,"
The bald one reminisces.
"What a jarring experience."

"They usually are," replied the sisters
Dripping in autonomy,
"All of them."

The quiet one picks up stones
To toss laterally through the air.
Shiny things, collected simply for
Being shiny.

"I used to be bored
But then I let myself forget all
The things I thought I knew."
The one whose hands smell like
Bagel shops grabs the hem of her
Petticoats to tuck into her mukluks.
"Ask her!"

The upside down one doesn't reply,
Red-faced from circumstantial gravity
And a body built against her will.

"So that's settled, then,"
Say I.
"We'll all stick around for tea."

Aliyah

Muted burgundy in the harsh sun
Reads overexposed like burnt summer skin
Out of place and difficult, I have brought myself
with me
And built shoes out of concrete
Wider than my hips

I hope I can show you
Where to gather raw materials and
How to beat them into life
Fire-forged, hissing in the cool waters
Of the Pacific